Classic Collection

THE WIZARD OF OZ

L. FRANK BAUM

Adapted by Ronne Randall • Illustrated by Liz Monahan

QEB Publishing

The Tornado

Dorothy lived with her Uncle Henry and Aunt Em on a farm in the middle of the huge Kansas prairies. Uncle Henry and Aunt Em both worked hard all day. Their skin was the same tone of gray as the dry, sunburned prairies that surrounded them. They never laughed and hardly ever smiled.

Dorothy, however, laughed a lot—especially at her little dog, Toto, with his silky black fur and merry black eyes. Dorothy loved him, and they played together every day.

Today, though, a big storm—a cyclone—was coming, and Dorothy, Aunt Em, and Uncle Henry were rushing to get to the storm cellar under their farmhouse, where they would be safe.

Toto was very frightened, and just as Dorothy was about to climb down the rickety cellar steps, he jumped out of her arms and tried to hide. Dorothy ran after him.

"Dorothy!" Aunt Em called, holding the cellar door open. "Come quickly! Run!" Dorothy grabbed Toto and tried to follow her aunt. But the house began to tremble and shake, and Dorothy fell to the floor.

Then an amazing thing happened. The whole house lifted up into the air and spun around! Terrified, Dorothy tightly held Toto. Hours passed, but the wind just kept wailing and the house kept whirling. Realizing there was nothing else to do but wait calmly, Dorothy crawled into her bed and eventually fell asleep.

The Munchkins

A big jolt woke Dorothy. When she looked outside, she could hardly believe her eyes. This wasn't Kansas! She had landed in the midst of a beautiful country filled with green grass and fruit trees. Suddenly, Dorothy saw some small people marching towards her.

"We, the Munchkins, welcome you to our land," said a man. "Thank you for killing our enemy."

"I haven't killed anyone!" Dorothy exclaimed.

"Your house did," said a woman. Sure enough, there were two feet sticking out from under Dorothy's house!

"I am the Good Witch of the North," said the woman. "The Wicked Witch of the East has been keeping the Munchkins as slaves, but you have freed them!"

"Have her silver shoes as your reward for saving us," said one of the Munchkins. "They are magical."

"You are in the Land of Oz," explained the Good Witch. There is still one Wicked Witch left—the Wicked Witch of the West, but you will be safe here with us."

"Thank you," Dorothy said, "but I just want to go home to Aunt Em and Uncle Henry. They will be so worried about me." And she began to cry.

"Maybe the Great Oz can help you," said the Good Witch. "The Wizard is more powerful than any of us and lives in the Emerald City. It's a long journey, but you just need to follow the Yellow Brick Road." The Witch pointed at the road and gave Dorothy a gentle kiss on the forehead for good luck.

Dorothy Meets the Scarecrow

Dorothy went into her house to collect food for the journey ahead. She changed into a clean dress and the Wicked Witch's silver shoes—they fitted perfectly!

As Dorothy and Toto walked along the Yellow Brick Road, many Munchkins came out to bow to them. They knew Dorothy had saved them from slavery, and they were very grateful. One of the Munchkins invited Dorothy to have supper and rest overnight in his home.

The next morning, as she and Toto continued on their journey, Dorothy stopped to rest beside a cornfield. A raggedy Scarecrow stood in the middle of the field.

As Dorothy gazed at the Scarecrow, she thought she saw it wink. Yes, it did. It winked! Then it spoke!

"Good day," he said. "Would you be so kind as to take this pole out of my back?"

"You spoke!" Dorothy said in surprise as she walked over and lifted the Scarecrow off the pole.

"Thank you very much," he said. "Now, who are you and where are you going?"

"My name is Dorothy, and I am going to the Emerald City to ask the Wizard to send me back home to Kansas."

"Maybe the Wizard could give me a brain," said the Scarecrow. "My head is stuffed with straw. I would love to have a brain so that people don't think I'm a fool."

"Why not come along, too?" said Dorothy. The Scarecrow nodded, and they set off.

Awhile later, the road became rough and uneven, with lots of holes and missing bricks. The farms were shabbier, too, with fewer fruit trees. The farther they went, the more dismal everything looked.

At lunchtime, Dorothy offered the Scarecrow some bread from her basket.

"No, thank you," he said politely. "I never get hungry. Besides, my mouth is only painted on."

The Scarecrow wanted to know all about Dorothy, so she told him about Kansas and about life with Aunt Em and Uncle Henry, who she missed terribly even though everything had been dull and gray.

The Scarecrow told her about his lonely life. At first, the crows were scared of him, but then an old crow came and sat on his shoulder. When the old crow realized the Scarecrow wasn't going to hurt him, he hopped down and started eating the corn. Soon a whole flock of crows came and joined him.

The old crow had told the Scarecrow that a brain was the only thing worth having, and he had longed for one ever since. Without one he felt like a fool and didn't think he was a very good Scarecrow.

Dorothy felt sorry for the Scarecrow and hoped the Wizard would be able to help him.

They continued walking, and toward evening they came to an empty cottage in the forest. Dorothy and Toto were both very tired, so they all went inside to rest.

The Tin Woodsman

Back on the Yellow Brick Road, Dorothy heard a groan. Through the trees, she saw a man made completely of tin, holding an ax. Dorothy and the Scarecrow stared in amazement, while Toto barked.

"I've been like this for a whole year," the man said in a creaking voice.

"How can we help you?" asked Dorothy.

"My joints have rusted and I can't move," the man explained. "There is an oil can in the cottage."

Dorothy ran to get the can and oiled the Tin Woodsman's rusty joints so that he could move again.

"You have certainly saved my life," he said with a sigh of relief. "How did you happen to be here?"

"We are going to the Emerald City to see the Great Oz," said Dorothy. "I want him to send me back home, and the Scarecrow wants to ask for a brain."

"Perhaps I could ask Oz for a heart!" the Tin Woodsman said. "I was once human, you see, and fell in love with a Munchkin girl. The girl's mother did not want me to marry her daughter, so she asked the Wicked Witch of the East to turn me to tin and take away my heart. Before I lost my heart, I was the happiest man in the world!"

Dorothy and the Scarecrow were pleased to have the Tin Woodsman for company, and he joined them on their journey to the Emerald City.

The Cowardly Lion

Dorothy and her friends continued through the forest. Dry branches and dead leaves covered the Yellow Brick Road, making it difficult to walk.

Every now and then they could hear wild animals growling, which made Dorothy's heart pound with fright. Toto stayed close beside her.

Suddenly, a terrible roar came from among the trees, and a huge Lion bounded out onto the road. With one blow of his big paw, he sent the Scarecrow spinning, and with another he knocked over the Tin Woodsman. Toto ran at the Lion, barking loudly, and he opened his mouth to bite the little dog.

"Don't you dare bite Toto!" cried Dorothy, slapping the Lion on the nose. "You should be ashamed of yourself. You're just a great big coward!"

To Dorothy's surprise, the Cowardly Lion hung his head. "You're right," he said. "I know that when I roar everyone gets frightened, but the truth is, whenever there is danger, my heart beats faster because I am scared."

"At least you have a heart!" said the Tin Woodsman. "I am going to ask the Great Oz for one."

"And I for a brain," said the Scarecrow.

"Do you think the Great Oz could give me courage?" asked the Cowardly Lion.

"Just as easily as he can send me back to Kansas," said Dorothy. "You are welcome to join us. By roaring you can scare away any wild beasts that come near."

That night, Dorothy and her friends camped out in the forest. All of Dorothy's bread was gone, so there was nothing for supper.

"I will kill a deer if you wish," the Cowardly Lion offered. "Then we will have some meat."

The Tin Woodsman begged the Lion not to kill any animals. "It would make me cry to see a helpless deer get hurt," he said, "and the tears would rust my jaw."

The Scarecrow gathered some nuts and filled Dorothy's basket so that she would not go hungry.

The next day, the Yellow Brick Road went through a dark, gloomy part of the forest.

"The Kalidahs live here," the Lion whispered. "They are monstrous beasts with bodies like bears, heads like tigers, and long, sharp claws. I'm terrified of them!"

They walked on carefully but had to stop when they came to a wide, deep ditch. How would they get across?

"I know!" said the Scarecrow. "If the Tin Woodsman chops down that tree, it will make a bridge for us."

The Woodsman got to work at once, and the tree soon fell with a crash. Just then they heard a loud growl.

"It's a Kalidah!" cried the Scarecrow. "Run!" They raced to the other side of the ditch, and the Tin Woodsman chopped away at the tree trunk. Just in time, it fell into the ditch, taking the Kalidah with it. They were all safe!

The Deadly Poppy Field

The next morning, the travelers came to a wide river at the edge of the forest. The Yellow Brick Road continued on the other side, where there were green meadows, flowers, and fruit trees.

The Tin Woodsman made a raft to carry them across the river, and they all climbed aboard. But the current in the middle of the river was so strong that it sent them rushing downstream. They could not get to the other side.

"I will swim to the shore," said the Cowardly Lion, "and pull the raft along with me."

When they were finally back on land, they realized that the current had pushed them far from the Yellow Brick Road. As they walked back along the riverbank, they passed a meadow full of bright red poppies.

"Aren't they beautiful?" said Dorothy. Suddenly, Dorothy felt so drowsy that she lay down and went to sleep right there by the side of the field. Toto fell asleep beside her. A moment later, the Lion fell asleep, too. Only the Scarecrow and the Tin Woodsman stayed awake, because they could not smell anything.

"We have to get our friends away from here!" said the Tin Woodsman. "These poppies are deadly. Their fragrance sends people and animals to sleep. If they stay here, they will sleep forever!"

The Lion was too heavy to lift, but together they managed to carry Dorothy and Toto away from the field. Would a fresh breeze wake them up?

The Queen of the Field Mice

While they watched over Dorothy and Toto, the Tin Woodsman and the Scarecrow saw a fierce wildcat chasing a little brown field mouse.

The Tin Woodsman felt sorry for the little mouse, so he raised his ax to frighten the wildcat away. The field mouse was very grateful.

"I am the Queen of the Field Mice," she said, "and in return for saving my life, we field mice will do anything you ask."

The Tin Woodsman and the Scarecrow asked if the mice could help rescue their friend the Lion. The mice squealed in terror, but the Tin Woodsman assured them that he was a Cowardly Lion who wouldn't hurt them, so they agreed to help.

The Tin Woodsman chopped some wood to make a wagon, while the mice fetched string.

The Woodsman used the string to harness the mice to the wagon, and they pulled it to the poppy field. They all helped lift the Lion into the wagon. Then, with everyone's help, they rolled the wagon back to Dorothy, who was now awake.

"Thank you so much for saving my friend the Lion," Dorothy said. "If you ever need us again, just whistle," said the Queen Field Mouse, handing Dorothy a tiny whistle.

To the Emerald City

When Dorothy and her friends set off again, they saw that all of the houses near the Yellow Brick Road were painted green. The people were dressed in green, too.

"We must be getting near the Emerald City," said Dorothy, "for everything is green."

By evening they were hungry and tired, so they knocked on a farmhouse door. The owner invited them to have supper with her family. They were amazed when Dorothy told them that they were going to see the Wizard of Oz.

"The Great Oz never lets anyone see him," said the woman's husband. "No one knows what he looks like."

"But we must see him," said Dorothy. "Otherwise our whole journey will have been for nothing."

They stayed at the farmhouse that night. The next morning, the travelers thanked the family and set off again. They soon reached the wall surrounding the Emerald City, where a small man stood guard at the gate. He was dressed from head to toe in green.

"We have come to see the Wizard," said Dorothy.

The man was astonished.

"It is many years since anyone has dared ask to see the Great Oz," he said. "But since I am the Guardian of the Gate, I must take you to him. First, though, you must put on these special eyeglasses. You must wear these day and night," he warned them. "Otherwise you will be blinded by the brightness of the Emerald City."

The Guardian took the four friends to the Wizard's palace. The soldier who let them in said that the Wizard would see them, but on their own and only one each day.

Dorothy went in first. The walls, floor, and ceiling of the throne room were covered with sparkling emeralds. A green marble throne sat in the middle of the room, and on it sat a giant head, with no arms, no legs…and no body! Just a head!

"I am Oz, the Great and Terrible," said a booming voice. "Who are you and why do you seek me?"

"Please," said Dorothy, "can you send me back to Kansas, where my Aunt Em and Uncle Henry are?"

"I will help you," said the Wizard, "but first you must help me and kill the Wicked Witch of the West!"

Dorothy burst into tears. "But I am just a little girl," she said. "I can't kill anyone, especially not a witch!"

The next day, it was the Scarecrow's turn. This time there was a beautiful woman on the glittering throne. She told the Scarecrow that if he wanted a brain, he would have to kill the Wicked Witch of the West first.

To the Tin Woodsman the Wizard took the shape of a terrible beast, and to the Lion he appeared as a fierce ball of fire. But his request was always the same: kill the Wicked Witch. After much discussion and many tears  from Dorothy, the four friends agreed there was only one thing to do. They must destroy the Witch.

The Journey to the West

The Guardian of the Gate showed Dorothy and her friends which way was West. Soon they had left the Emerald City far behind and were in the rough, hilly country of the West.

The Wicked Witch of the West had only one eye, but that eye was like a telescope and could see everywhere. When she saw Dorothy and her friends on her land, she was furious and set out to destroy them.

First she summoned a pack of wolves by blowing on a silver whistle around her neck. "Tear those strangers to pieces!" she ordered.

The wolves attacked, but luckily the Tin Woodsman saw them coming. He chopped off the wolves' heads one by one with his ax.

Next, the Wicked Witch ordered a flock of crows to peck out their eyes. But the crows were frightened by the Scarecrow and flew away.

The Witch, angrier than ever, sent out a swarm of bees to sting Dorothy and her friends to death. The Scarecrow saw the bees approaching and had an idea. He told the Tin Woodsman to take out his straw so that Dorothy, Toto, and the Lion could hide underneath it. When the bees arrived, the Tin Woodsman was the only one they could sting, and they soon broke their sharp stings on his hard metal shell.

They all helped stuff the Scarecrow's straw back into his clothes and set off once again.

The Winged Monkeys

The Witch had only one thing left to use. She put on her golden cap and called her most powerful helpers, the Winged Monkeys. She could call on them only three times, and this would be the third time.

When the Monkeys arrived, the Witch said, "Destroy them all except the Lion. I will hold him prisoner."

The Monkeys caught the Tin Woodsman first. Lifting him high, they dropped him on some rocks, where his body lay battered and broken. They caught the Scarecrow next and took out all of his stuffing. Then they tied up the Lion and flew him back to the Witch's courtyard. But when they saw the mark of the Good Witch's kiss on Dorothy's forehead, they dared not harm her. Instead they took her to the Witch.

The Witch was also afraid of the mark and of the silver shoes, but she soon realized that Dorothy was unaware of their magic powers. She decided to make Dorothy her slave and find a way to steal them.

Dorothy worked hard, sweeping and scrubbing, and began to fear she would never make it home. One day, in an attempt to snatch the shoes, the Witch tricked Dorothy into tripping. This made Dorothy so angry that she flung a bucket of water at the Witch. Then an amazing thing happened: the Wicked Witch of the West melted away, leaving only a puddle behind!

The Rescue

After mopping up the puddle, Dorothy rushed to the courtyard to free the Lion. Then they called all of the Witch's slaves together to tell them that they were also free. They were called the Winkies, and the land had been theirs before the Wicked Witch had captured them.

"If only the Scarecrow and the Tin Woodsman were with us," said the Lion, "I would be so happy!"

"We'll help you find them!" said the Winkies. They formed a search party and quickly found the Tin Woodsman's broken body. Tenderly, they carried him back to the Witch's castle where Dorothy and the Lion were anxiously waiting.

The Winkies' best tinsmiths repaired the Tin Woodsman's body, and they fashioned a brand-new ax for him out of shimmering gold and silver. They found the Scarecrow's clothes, which they stuffed with fresh, clean straw. The two friends were both as good as new!

It was time for Dorothy and her friends to go back to the Emerald City and tell the Great Wizard that they had done what he'd asked. The Winkies wished them well and gave them presents for their journey: golden collars for Toto and the Lion; a sparkling bracelet for Dorothy; a silver oil can for the Tin Woodsman; and a gold-tipped cane for the Scarecrow.

Dorothy went to the kitchen to get some food for the journey. There she also found the Witch's golden cap.

"That looks pretty," she said. "I think I'll wear it."

There was no Yellow Brick Road to lead them from the Witch's castle back to the Emerald City. The travelers had to find their way through fields of wildflowers, and before long they were lost.

They wandered for days, sleeping under the stars, hoping to see something that would show them the way. Finally, too exhausted to go any farther, they sat down on the grass.

"Do you think the Field Mice know the way to the Emerald City?" Dorothy wondered.

She blew her whistle, and within minutes there was the patter of tiny feet. Soon they were surrounded by little brown mice.

"Can you tell us the way to the Emerald City?" Dorothy asked them.

The Queen stepped forward. "Of course," she said. "But it is far away. The Witch's golden cap gives its wearer three wishes. Summon the Winged Monkeys, and they will help you."

When Dorothy realized that the golden cap was more than just a pretty hat, she was doubly glad that she had taken it. Dorothy called for the Monkeys. They arrived very quickly and agreed to Dorothy's request. Holding the four friends in their arms, the Monkeys rose up into the air and flew off. Very soon they were all in the Emerald City.

The Discovery of Oz, the Terrible

After a long wait at the Wizard's palace, a soldier finally took them into the throne room. A booming voice said, "I am Oz, the Great and Terrible. Why do you seek me?"

"The Wicked Witch is dead," said Dorothy. "Now you must keep your promises."

"Er…come back tomorrow," said the voice, a little shakily.

"Don't make us wait!" roared the Lion, so loudly that Toto jumped, knocking over a screen. To everyone's amazement, a little old man stood there, shaking.

"Who are you?" asked Dorothy in surprise.

"I am Oz, the Great and Terrible," said the man with a sheepish look. "But you can call me Oz. As you can see, I am not a Wizard at all. I am just an ordinary man."

"You mean you've been fooling us all along?" Dorothy asked.

"Yes," admitted Oz guiltily. "I was once a magician, so I know how to do lots of tricks. The Emerald City isn't even green. It just looks that way through the glasses. I used to fly hot-air balloons, and when the people saw me coming through the clouds, they thought I was a great Wizard. Please don't reveal my secret."

"But how will you keep your promises to us?" asked the Scarecrow.

"Come back tomorrow, and I will do my best," said Oz.

Oz Keeps his Promises

The next day, the Scarecrow was the first to go in to see Oz. He was very eager to get his brain.

"I will have to remove your head," said Oz, "but I will put it back again, and it will be better than before."

He took off the Scarecrow's head and replaced the straw with bran. When he put it back on the Scarecrow, he said, "Now you have a fine bran-new brain."

"Thank you so much!" said the Scarecrow. He rushed out to tell his friends how much wiser he felt.

Next, it was the Tin Woodsman's turn to get his heart. Oz opened a drawer and took out a lovely red velvet heart stuffed with sawdust.

"Is it a kind heart?" asked the Tin Woodsman.

"Very," said Oz, and he cut a small hole in the Tin Woodsman's chest, just big enough to hold the new heart.

When the Lion came in, Oz took a green bottle down from a shelf and poured some liquid into a bowl.

"Drink that," he told the Lion.

"What is it?" asked the Lion.

"Well," said Oz, "if it were inside you, it would be courage—because courage always comes from the inside."

The Lion drank all of the liquid and said he felt very brave. Oz was pleased with himself.

"How can I help playing tricks," he said to himself, "when everyone wants me to do things that can't be done? But there's still one problem: how can I get Dorothy back to Kansas?"

Dorothy was longing to go home, but Oz needed time to think. At last he sent for her.

"I have a plan," he said. "I came here in a balloon, and I'm sure we can leave in one. We can make one out of silk—there is plenty of silk in the palace. We'll fill it with hot air, and it will float us home."

"Us?" said Dorothy. "Are you coming with me?"

"Yes," replied Oz. "I am tired of being shut up in this palace. I can't go anywhere, because if I did, everyone would realize that I am not a real Wizard. I would much rather go back to Kansas with you and join the circus."

For the next three days, Dorothy helped Oz make the balloon. When it was finished, they attached a big clothes basket to it. Oz announced that he was going to visit a brother wizard who lived in the clouds and that Dorothy was going with him. A big crowd came to see them off.

"While I am away," Oz announced, "the Scarecrow will rule over you. Obey him as you would me. Now come, Dorothy, climb into the basket."

The hot air was making the balloon rise and tug at its ropes, but Dorothy wouldn't leave without Toto, who had chased a cat into the crowd.

Suddenly, there was a loud SNAP! The balloon's ropes broke, and Oz went floating up into the sky. Dorothy watched helplessly as Oz and the balloon drifted off without her.

Setting Out for the South

Now that Oz was gone, Dorothy wondered how she would ever get back home. She used the golden cap to call the Winged Monkeys, but the Monkey King said they could not go to Kansas.

Dorothy didn't know what to do until a soldier in the Wizard's palace mentioned that Glinda, the Good Witch of the South who ruled over the Quadlings, might be able to help.

Dorothy and her friends set off for the South and traveled for days. They went through a thick, dark forest, with frightening fighting trees. Then they climbed over a smooth, high wall and into a land where the ground was as white and shiny as a dinner plate, and the tiny people were made of fragile china.

In another forest, they came upon a crowd of noisy animals having a meeting. When the animals saw the Lion, they welcomed him.

"You have come just in time to save us from our enemy," they said. The enemy was a huge spider that crawled through the forest, eating animals big and small. Now full of courage, the Lion crept up bravely to the sleeping spider and, with one blow, knocked off its head!

"You need not worry about your enemy anymore," he told the animals. All of the beasts bowed to the Lion and said he was now their King. The Lion promised to come back and rule over them once Dorothy was on her way.

The Hammerheads

After leaving the forest, the travelers came to a steep hill, covered from top to bottom with pieces of rock. As they began to climb, a huge hammer-shaped head popped up over a rock and said, "Stay back! This is our hill, and no one is allowed to cross it!"

"We're crossing this hill whether you like it or not," said the Scarecrow, moving forward boldly.

As quick as a flash, the huge head shot forward as its neck stretched out. It hit the Scarecrow hard, sending him tumbling down the hill. Laughter rang out around them, and suddenly hundreds more Hammerheads appeared, one behind each rock. The Lion dashed up the hill, but before he could get very far, another head shot forward and sent him rolling backward.

"Fighting these horrid heads is useless," the Lion said as he got up.

"But how will we get over the hill?" Dorothy asked.

"Call the Winged Monkeys," said the Tin Woodsman. "You still have one wish left."

So Dorothy put on the golden cap and sent for the Winged Monkeys. They were there in an instant and swiftly carried Dorothy and her friends south to Quadling country. The land seemed rich and happy, with fields of ripening grain and rippling brooks. All of the fences, houses, and bridges were painted bright red. It seemed like a happy place.

Meeting Glinda the Good Witch

The travelers knocked on a farmhouse door and were welcomed in by the farmer's wife. She was kind and generous and gave Dorothy and her friends a good dinner. Then she told them how to get to the castle of Glinda the Good Witch.

When they got to the castle, Glinda saw them at once. She was beautiful, with flowing red hair and kind blue eyes, and she sat on a throne of rubies.

Dorothy told Glinda everything that had happened, starting with the tornado.

"Of course I will help you," said Glinda. "But I will need the golden cap." Dorothy had already used its magic three times and was happy to part with it. Glinda then told them how she would use her three commands.

"I will ask the Winged Monkeys to take the Scarecrow back to the Emerald City, where he will be a wonderful ruler," she said. "Tin Woodsman, you will go back to the Land of the Winkies, where you will be a wise and goodhearted ruler. Finally, the Winged Monkeys will take the Lion back to the forest, where he will be the King of the Beasts."

"Then what will happen to the golden cap?" asked Dorothy.

"I will give it to the King of the Winged Monkeys," said Glinda. "Then he and his band will be freed from its power forever."

"But what about me?" wondered Dorothy.

Dorothy's Wish Is Granted

The Scarecrow, the Tin Woodsman, and the Lion had had their wishes granted and would now be rulers of their own lands, but Dorothy was still puzzled.

"How will I get back to Kansas?" she asked.

"The silver shoes will take you there," Glinda replied. "If you had known their power, you could have gone home the first day you got here."

"But then I never would have gotten my brain!" said the Scarecrow.

"Nor I my heart!" said the Tin Woodsman.

"And I would have been a coward forever," said the Lion.

"That is all true," said Dorothy. "I am glad that I have helped, but now that you are all happy, what I want most of all is to go back to Kansas."

"The silver shoes have wonderful powers," said Glinda. "All you have to do is click your heels three times and tell the shoes where to take you."

So Dorothy would at last get her wish. She hugged and kissed each of her friends. They were all very sad to say goodbye— but they were happy for each other, too. Glinda stepped down from her throne to give Dorothy a goodbye kiss. Then, taking Toto in her arms and saying one last farewell, Dorothy clicked her heels three times and said, "Take me home!"

Home Again

Instantly, Dorothy and Toto were lifted up and went whirling through the air. Everything was happening so quickly that all Dorothy could hear or feel was the wind rushing past her ears.

The silver shoes took just three steps and then stopped so suddenly that Dorothy found herself rolling over and over on the grass before she even knew where she was.

Finally, Dorothy sat up and looked around.

"Oh, good gracious!" she cried—for she could see that she was on the wide Kansas prairie. Right in front of her was a new farmhouse—the one that Uncle Henry had built after the tornado carried off the old one. And there, milking the cows in the farmyard just as he always had, was Uncle Henry himself. Toto jumped out of Dorothy's arms and ran toward him, barking joyfully.

Dorothy stood up, wondering where the silver shoes had gone. At that moment, Aunt Em came out of the house, holding a watering can. When she saw Dorothy, she dropped the watering can and ran to her with her arms open wide.

"Oh, my darling child!" she cried, tightly hugging Dorothy and covering her face with kisses. "Where in the world have you been?"

Dorothy thought her heart would burst with happiness. "I've been in the Land of Oz," she replied. "Oh, Aunt Em, I'm so happy to be home!"

About the author

Lyman Frank Baum was born in New York in 1856.
Lyman grew up in a wealthy family and pursued many
careers. They varied from actor, to poultry breeder,
to dime store owner. He married his wealthy wife in 1882
while touring with the performance of his play *The Maid
of Arran*. It was her mother, suffragist Matilda Josylyn Gage,
who encouraged Lyman to publish his imaginative stories.
His first novel was published in 1899, and *The Wizard of Oz*
was published the following year. It was so popular that
readers demanded more tales from Oz, so Lyman
completed 14 books in a series. He died in 1919.

Other titles in the *Classic Collection* series:

Alice's Adventures in Wonderland • *Heidi* • *Little Women*
Pinocchio • *The Three Musketeers* • *Treasure Island*
20,000 Leagues Under the Sea

Editors: Joanna Pocock and Vicky Garrard • Designer: Andrea Mills

Copyright © QEB Publishing 2012

First published in the United States in 2012 by
QEB Publishing, Inc.
3 Wrigley, Suite A
Irvine, CA 92618

www.qed-publishing.co.uk

A CIP record for this book is available from the Library of Congress.

ISBN 978 1 60992 301 3

Printed in China